WELCOME TO
Kite Day

Today is Kite Day.

1

Dave and Jean made their own kites.

Dave's kite is beautiful. Jean's kite is plain.

The kites soar up into the deep blue sky.
They dip and dive in the wind.

Then a strong gust breaks Dave's kite in half.
"Oh no!" Dave cries. The tail of his kite drifts
to the ground.

Jean's kite flies higher and higher,
like a sturdy brown bird.
Finally, she reels it in.

"Next time, let's make a kite together,"
Jean tells Dave.

"Okay," says Dave. "Our kite will be strong *and* beautiful."